FABER NEW POE

IN THE SAME SERIES

1 – FIONA BENSON
2 – TOBY MARTINEZ DE LAS RIVAS
3 – HEATHER PHILLIPSON
4 – JACK UNDERWOOD

Jack Underwood

---

ff

faber and faber

First published in 2009
by Faber and Faber Ltd
Bloomsbury House
74–77 Great Russell Street
London WC1B 3DA

Typeset by Faber & Faber Ltd
Printed in England by T. J. International Ltd, Padstow, Cornwall

ACKNOWLEDGEMENTS

My thanks to Sam Riviere, Hannah Bagshaw, Lavinia Greenlaw, Maura Dooley, George Szirtes, Maurice Riordan, Matthew Hollis and my parents; to the Society of Authors for an Eric Gregory Award and the Arts and Humanities Research Council; to *Poetry London*, *The Rialto* and *Smiths Knoll* where some of these poems have previously appeared.

A CIP record for this book
is available from the British Library

ISBN 978–0–571–24998–5

2 4 6 8 10 9 7 5 3 1

Contents

Weasel

So Weasel, it has come to this;
to your thighs like tall glasses of milk,
your biscuit hair,
eyes that are like any kind of deep water.
It has come to those coiled, snaking guts
we had when we were younger still –
those balled-up sock guts of an afternoon
stolen back from college.
It has come to the spastic, ticking urges
rising through skin at the simplest
repositioning of your weasel hips,
or the one in twenty-seven kisses
I might land about your mouth,
of the right temperature and diction.

Was I even hungry once for eating?
Were you ever not the end to all fasts?

Theology

He tried to think about the zoo,
the bird he'd seen with an anvil head,
slinking lizards in the reptile house.
It had been a good day.

But he remembered the panther enclosure
where he had waited for thirty minutes,
staring up at a dark hut hidden in trees.
Suppose there was no panther.

Maths

To commemorate the grand bazaar
the king is given a prize goat (x)
that is one and a half metres high.
Given that a prize goat eats
ten square yards of grass a day,
how long should the leash (y)
be tied so the prize goat can roam free
and feed until the next bazaar?

To the man who can give an answer
in yards and show his working,
goes the talcum hand of the virgin princess
who is also one and a half metres high.

Men come. One brings a ball of string
and a cauliflower to show he is both wise
and humble, another swings a bag of seeds,
two brothers flex their matching red braces.

So the suitors measure, scribble, compare
their feats of mind, strength and faith.
Bunting feathers the eaves, a local man
juggles numbers through the streets
dressed in the fleece and horns of a buck.
The princess bites her lip, her hair plaited
with ribbons the colours of her country.
Meanwhile the goat goes hungry.

Bonnie 'Prince' Billy

He is also singing how I will split
the atom and leave it for you cleaved
in two on the breadboard like an apple,
will peel your star-sign off the sky,
dissolve and serve it hot in a cup.

He sings how ugly and complex
I have become, sitting at the table,
gripping the stupidity of wood.

He sings how deeply I am weakened
by a single drip of water
falling from the end of your nose
and soaking into my jeans
like an excuse into the wider scheme of things.

Your horse

has arrived and is bending himself into the room,
refolding his legs. I knuckle his nose,
which reminds me of the arm of a chair.

He is talking low and steady,
rolling back an eye towards his chestnut brain.
Man-words are climbing his long throat.

I show him to the bathroom
and he is embarrassed. Next he is hoofing
through your photo album.

There are more of me, than of him.
We are crunching on polo mints together
and remembering the way your body used to move.

Migration

In the centre of her nation's flag
is a big, milky, onion, *God is sustenance!*
on a ribbon round its middle.

She tells me it is customary
for the guest to provide meat for the pot.
All her brothers nod.

Tonight her American boyfriend
has brought his hunk of steak.
I will try the border again tomorrow,

but not before it's my turn
and I must break the neck of a bird
that has flown here for the winter.

Hannah-loo

Sam Lynch lent me a gypsy dollar to cut our first record
at the hollow shack off Memoir Street.
In those days, no one wore haircuts and jeans were for working men.
There was me, Nic and Joe on bass and the song was 'Hannah-loo'.
We took our mark from country, but played it fast, on the back beat
like this – *bum tappa tum tap* – until we got tired.
Joe slept with one hand in buttermilk, to keep it supple, the other
for plucking, in sand, or was it dirt, or the other way around?
Anyway, the point is, we tried things out.
Nic's brothers made up a whole bomber crew,
though strictly that wasn't allowed. They slammed the can
fourth time up so she had to work the horses herself.
I swear when she hit those drums she was thinking about bombs
    dropping,
the foreign batteries, but I never told Joe. He was due for call-up.
Me, I played guitar steady and hard, but kept my fingers moving.
The paper said my right hand was a river, my left hand a salmon,
working upstream. I liked that, so I put it on our posters.
I think I have one somewhere, if you can spare another minute?

And what do you do?

Write codenames, military mainly.
'Operation blunt-tongue', that was me,
'spirit-hat', 'yard-mile', them too.

I'm jacking it in next month:
civvy street, open shirt, slip-on shoes.
I've a job lined-up in colours.

How about 'burnt viscose', 'black jam'?
Would you paint your hall with 'easy money'?
These days there's little left to call.

What beautiful blue eyes you have.

Gottlieb

If I leave you here you will surely die,
as sure as the worms will find your pockets.

I'll carry you beyond that ridge.
Which is more than reasonable.
You are a heavy man and I have my own
skin to lift. Leave behind your letters
to your puppy kids and rabbit wife.
I cannot risk the extra weight.

In the morning you may be found.
Your eyes will be filled with water, daylight
and the yellow beaks of gulls.

Ice-cream

The message got through that tanks
from the Army of our Great Nation
were *only weeks away*.

We had four frozen horses left to eat,
so saving the fine French chair from the fire,
took turns to sit and pull hot steaks apart
with dirty hands.

The message never got through that tanks
from the Army of our Great Nation
were hollowed-out by shells, thumped,
just inside the border.

We received no word, no supplies, no orders,
but picked our teeth in secret, at night,
the fires growing dimmer, the rats more brave.

In a month all that remained of the horses,
the chair, were spindles of legs
holding up the useless dream;
a message getting through that summer
was *only weeks away*, the cold we felt inside
was really just relief and ice-cream.

Brother Hen

has built a new coop
high as himself, on dog-proof stilts
in worm-rich earth. He reaches his long arm
through the chicken door, explores,
finger-tipping for egg warm shapes.
He lifts one out, careful and astonished,
as if retrieving a voice from an oven.

I tell my Brother Hen I have a system
for the soft-boiled, about my trick with salt
under the lid, but he knows best that an egg
should not be cajoled or spooned, but is
an internal balancing act, a system of its own,
to be held aloft, considered, as an example
of grace and the duty of hens.

for Tom

How shall I say this?

I was sick as worms and knew it
from my aching balls to my heavy tongue.
I lay on the forest floor, the beetles
rolling their dung loud as boulders.

You should not be up here alone
she said and pushed to my chin
the bulbous lump of a fig, pressed
its cool suede skin to the side of my face.

We rolled it together, to the edge of my mouth.
A shock of macaws took off,
colour rushed to our cheeks as sap foamed
from the wound of a nearby stump.

I had never eaten . . .
How shall I say this?
I had never eaten from a woman's hand
nor had she fed before such fruit to a man.

Currency

George's mother has dough-hands: round, pale, pillow-fingers.
Her apron is stiff with potato starch and she smells of sweetcorn.
The backs of her arms are shiny with work sweat.
His father calls me *eldest* (though he has older children)
and introduces me to the mayor who shows me wine purpled teeth
then six shrapnel scars, one in the shape of a fig leaf.
The Bandettas come down from the hills, ride me on their scooters
to the river where we play at drowning each other. In leather jackets,
they pose for my camera, taking turns to wear my sunglasses.
I am dropped back in town for the feast and evening dances.
Children hide and squeal in night clothes. The mayor
in his old blue uniform, fingers his medals like a farmer testing good soil.
George leads Sabrina by the chin to the fig orchards behind the church,
so I sit on a hay bale, talking for his sister. She touches my left palm
to her right kidney, asks in a neat, foreign whisper 'I have been waiting
for you?' What else can I say but 'Yes' and 'For me'?

Wilderbeast

In the wilderness the devil came to me:
big antique horns, a swinging red dick
and my father's angry voice.

He offered me grapes, a puckered teat
loose with wine and milk. I spat.
And he spat back, my mother's maiden name.

I pressed on, urged my feet. Satan changed tack;
swam me in sensation: my first time drunk,
the heat of a well spun lie, boyhood

glimpsed between a hairdresser's breasts,
the smell of shampoo and cigarette breath.
Then from a tuck in his arse he pulled rain

and a chip-shop queue, the taste of shandy,
wet football boots dangled by the laces,
acorns and conkers tumbling from their spouts.

I gave a shout, a kind of grief escaping
and from astride his chin appeared
two slim girl's legs, akimbo his beard.

He opened his ripe mouth, folded his tongue back
and in, wriggling pleasure from himself,
stamping it out on the bare earth, braying.

I felt hunger folding in my gut.
The devil swung his hips, each jerk giving birth
to a pair of round, pert tits. *I am a good man!*

I railed and each flesh sack withered and slapped
on the ground, sizzled on the grit-heat of rock.
I heard waves, an ocean then. But it was Satan

shushing with a four-knuckled finger to his lips.
A breeze faltered and caught over, sea birds swung
in long arcs. The devil leaned in and touched me,

quietly, here and then here.
Softly he drew a perfect circle on the ground
bid me dream my mortal desire inside it.

I took out a photograph of you my love.
Showed him grace: fixed and flattened,
wrapped in a scarf and coat last week,

when the camera pinned you to the sea
and I watched it happen from behind the lens;
my breath holding you there a moment.

I showed the devil your photo and he wept.
Flies fell buzzing from his cheeks.
You tempted and turned him

and the sun strained to look
as the perfect circle became a pool of water,
hardened into a mirror,

the mirror I've been staring into since,
in our bathroom, in our flat,
with the wilderness of seconds between us.

Toad

Toad, I have told you already,
this is not your house. Why do you insist
on staying there under the sink?
You cannot eat the soap like that,
it makes your insides sick.

I remember toad, the shed we used to sit in.
How, in the fizzing light of a twenty-watt bulb
you were moved to unbutton love, to turn out
your pockets and inspect the lint and sand
in the oil palm of your toad hand.
You were friendly in the sawdust then,
your toad face wide as the brim of your hat.

You cannot eat the soap like that.
Toad, it makes my insides sick.

Certain

Nothing before had seemed so potent
and self-contained –
surely the onion was beautiful.

Its hung cloud of acid worked
in his nose and throat
as the knife bisected

like a maker of names passing
between twins, calling one half *Perfect*
the other also *Perfect*.